RYAN G. MCCLARREN

RADIATION AND YOU

ORION SCIENTIFIC PUBLISHING
COLLEGE STATION, TEXAS
USA

ISBN 978-0692741542

PUBLISHED BY ORION SCIENTIFIC PUBLISHING
COLLEGE STATION, TEXAS
USA

DRRYANMC.COM

First printing, July 2016

To Beatrix, Flannery, Lowry, and Cormac

What are atoms?

Everything around you is made of atoms: the air you breathe, your body, this book you are holding. You cannot see atoms, though, because they are so small. Different types of atoms make up the different items around you. For example, hydrogen and oxygen atoms make up water. Other atoms that you may have heard of are silver, gold, or iron atoms.

Atoms are the building blocks of nature, but they are made of even smaller things called protons, neutrons, and electrons. An atom has protons and neutrons in the middle part, called a nucleus, with electrons flying around outside the nucleus. The part outside the nucleus, where the electrons are, is called the electron cloud. The number of electrons in the cloud is the same as the number of protons in the nucleus. Atoms with the same number of protons are called elements. For example, all gold atoms have 79 protons, but could have any number of neutrons. Sometimes you will see a number after the atom's name: this tells you the total number of neutrons and protons in the nucleus. For instance, gold-197 has 79 protons and 118 neutrons in the nucleus.

In your body alone there are over 10,000,000,000,000,000,000,000 atoms!

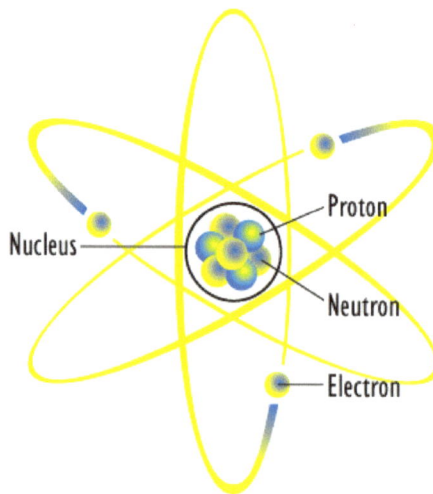

This is an atom: it has a nucleus of protons and neutrons surrounded by electrons.

Nucleus

Proton

Neutron

Electron

Scientists have thought that atoms make up everything for thousands of years but have not been able to see them with a microscope until recently. Even when scientists take pictures of atoms, they cannot see past the electron cloud. This makes the atoms look like circles in a picture.

Protons and electrons have what is called a charge. These charges are responsible for electricity.

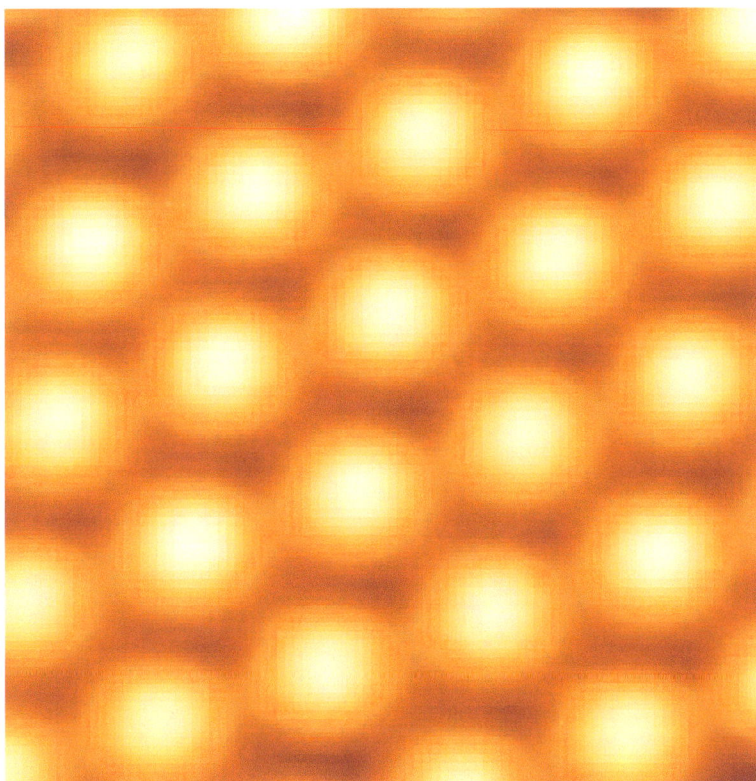

Over 2000 years ago, the ancient Greek philosopher Democritus thought that all matter was made of a basic building block he called atoms.

This is a picture of atoms of the element silicon using a scanning tunneling microscope.

Radiation and radioactivity

Some atoms will break up and change by shooting protons and neutrons out of its nucleus. Atoms that break down like this are called radioactive, and the things they shoot out are called radiation. When a radioactive atom changes this way, scientists say that it decays into another atom.

Alpha radiation is a type of radiation where two protons and two neutrons are ejected from the nucleus of the atom. This type of radiation is used in smoke detectors. Alpha radiation can have a lot of energy, but it can be stopped by something as thin as a piece of paper or your skin.

Beta radiation happens when a nucleus shoots out an electron and turns a neutron into a proton. This type of radiation is used to tell how long ago extinct animals lived. The electrons from beta radiation are a little harder to stop than alpha radiation. Beta radiation can be stopped by an aluminum can, like the kind that soup comes in.

Gamma radiation happens when a nucleus has too much energy (scientists called this an excited nucleus). To get rid of the energy, the nucleus shoots out light called a gamma ray. Scientists use gamma radiation to make food safer through irradiation. Gamma rays are hard to stop and can go through concrete (like that used to make roads) and heavy metals like lead.

There is another type of radiation called x-ray radiation. This is like gamma radiation, except in this case the electron has too much energy and it shoots out light. Doctors use x-rays to see if a person has a broken bone.

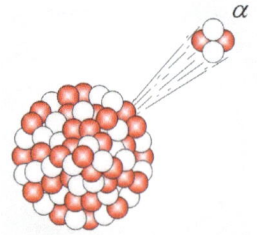

Alpha radiation happens when the nucleus shoots out two protons and two neutrons.

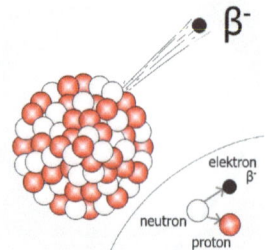

Beta radiation happens when the nucleus shoots out an electron and turns a neutron into a proton.

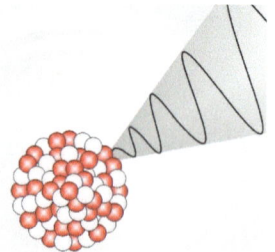

Gamma radiation happens when the nucleus has too much energy. The nucleus then releases light.

Some common uses of radiation

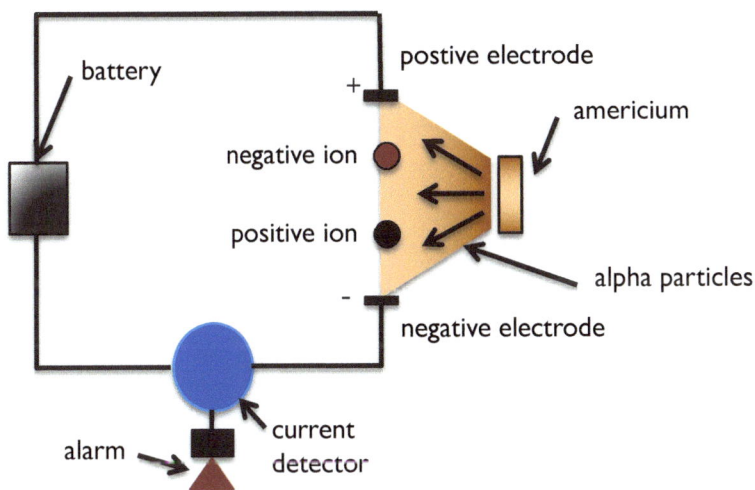

Outside of a household
smoke detector.

Radiation has many uses in your life. Smoke detectors use
radiation to tell us if there is a fire. Inside a smoke detector
there is a radioactive atom called americium. Americium shoots
out protons and neutrons as alpha radiation. When there is
smoke, the protons and neutrons are blocked, and the smoke
detector makes a loud sound to let us know there is a fire.

When smoke blocks radia-
tion, the alarm goes off in a
smoke detector.

battery

postive electrode

+

negative ion

americium

positive ion

alpha particles

-

negative electrode

alarm

current
detector

Here is a picture of the
americium from inside
a smoke detector. The
colorful part in the middle
is the americium: the
americium is smaller than a
grain of sand.

Doctors and nurses also use radiation to see inside our body. X-rays are a type of light that comes from electrons having too much energy. These x-rays can go right through skin but not bone. This lets doctors take pictures of the inside of your body. X-rays are also used by dentists to check your teeth. Doctors can also put radioactive atoms in a person's body to see parts of our body that are not bone.

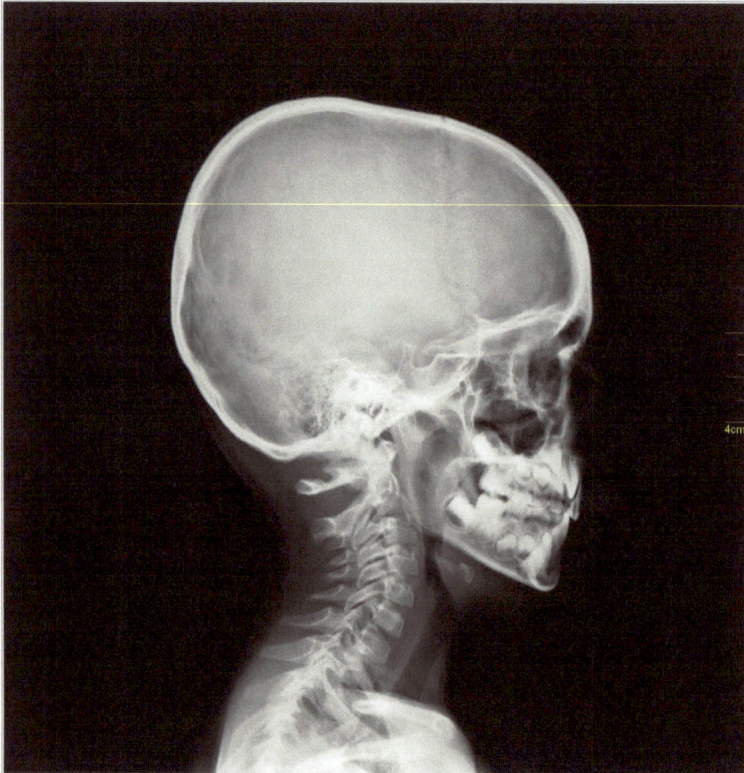

This is a picture of a human brain taken using a procedure called a PET scan. In a PET scan radioactive atoms are injected into the body to show doctors how a person's brain is working.

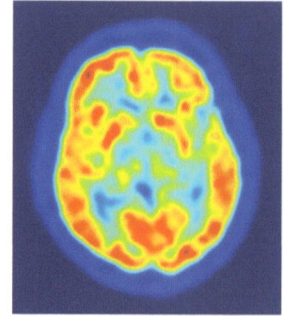

X-ray picture of a human head and neck. You can see all the bones and teeth with an x-ray.

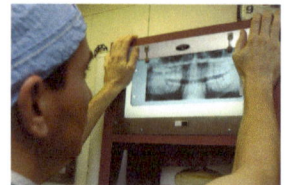

This dentist is looking at an x-ray of a person's teeth to check for cavities or other problems.

Radiation is also used to treat diseases. One sickness, called cancer, is often treated using radiation. Some types of radioactive medicine are injected, like a shot with a needle, right into the sick part of the body.

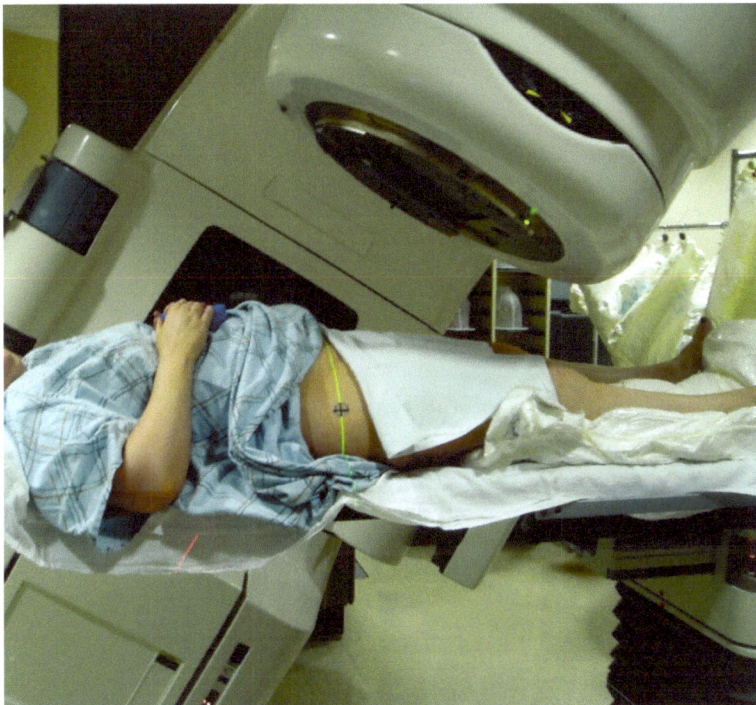

This woman is getting radiation beamed into a sick part of her body by this large machine.

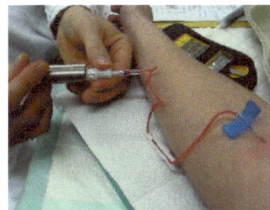

This patient is having a radioactive medicine injected into her body. Notice that the medicine is inside a lead shield in the nurse's hand.

Radiation is natural

Radiation occurs all around us. Some comes from natural radioactive atoms in the dirt. The atoms of uranium, thorium, and potassium are the most common of these. Also, the food you eat contains some radioactive atoms as well. Bananas, kidney beans, spinach, and some nuts have radioactive atoms in them.

Radiation also comes to Earth from space. When stars far, far away explode, they create radiation that travels all the way to Earth. The air and clouds in the sky help to block much of the radiation, but some reaches the ground. When you fly in an airplane, more of this radiation hits you because there is less air and clouds above you to block the radiation.

A banana contains a small number of radioactive potassium atoms.

In an airplane you are closer to outer space and the radiation that comes from space.

This uranium mine in Utah contains natural radioactive atoms.

The dangers of radiation

Radiation can be useful, but too much of it can hurt you. That is why doctors and nurses leave the room when giving you an x-ray: so they don't get any radiation. If a person gets too much radiation at one time, it can make that person very sick. Wherever there is a radiation danger, there will be signs and other warnings. As long as you follow the directions, you will be safe.

In some parts of the world, the radioactive atom radon is produced naturally in the dirt and rocks. Radon can get into the air in a house through the ground. The radon can be breathed in by people and can make them sick. You can test your home for radon with a kit you buy at the hardware store. If a house has radon in it, there are ways to remove it safely.

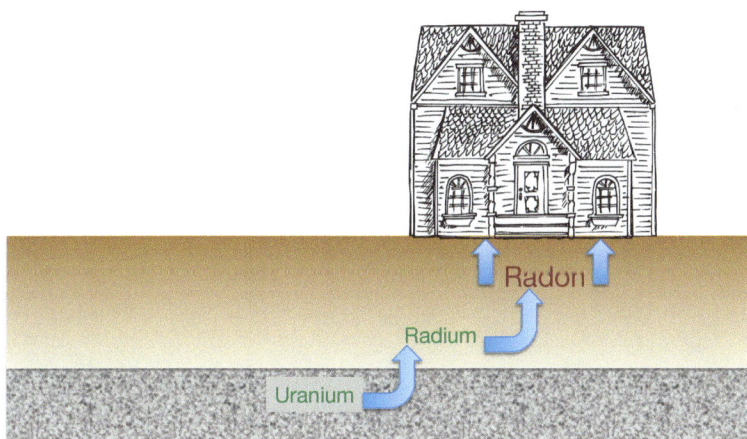

When you see a radiation warning sign, make sure to follow its directions.

Radon comes from uranium in the bedrock below ground. The uranium turns into radium and then radon. Radon is a gas that can leak into homes through the bottom of the house.

This is a radon test kit. It can measure radon in a house, to make sure radon is not leaking into a house from the ground.

Astronauts and radiation

Radiation can be dangerous for astronauts. In space, astronauts do not have the air and clouds of the Earth to protect them from radiation. Most of the radiation in space comes from the sun. The farther astronauts are from the Earth, the more radiation they get. Even near the Earth, astronauts need to have shields in the space ship to protect them from radiation. Shields can make a spaceship heavy and harder to launch into space. To go far from Earth, bigger shields are needed.

When he walked on the moon, Buzz Aldrin was one of the first people to be in the radiation of space far from the Earth.

The International Space Station has shielding to protect astronauts from too much radiation.

When astronauts went to the moon, it was the first time that people were exposed to the radiation of space away from the Earth. The short trip to the moon was not long enough to give the astronauts too much radiation. If people are going to travel to other planets, engineers need to solve the problem of protecting the astronauts without making the spaceships too heavy to launch into space.

While on the moon, astronauts did experiments to measure the radiation that hits the moon.

Radiation and bones

How do people know how long ago extinct animals lived? The answer is radiation and carbon dating. Carbon is a type of atom that is very common in bones and in every living thing. Some atoms of carbon are radioactive. When those atoms of carbon shoot out an electron (this is beta radiation), it becomes a nitrogen atom. The radioactive carbon atoms decay into nitrogen like a kind of clock. When an animal is alive, it adds new radioactive carbon to its body by breathing and eating; this stops when the animal dies. By looking at the amount of radioactive carbon in a fossil, scientists can tell how long ago the animal lived. The less radioactive carbon in the bones, the longer ago the animal lived. This is one of the ways scientists know how long ago the animals like sabertooth tigers and wooly mammoths lived.

Carbon dating can only be used on animal bones less than 50,000 years old. Other radioactive atoms are used to date bones of animals that lived longer ago. To figure out how long ago dinosaurs lived, the age of the rocks around the dinosaur's bones is measured using uranium.

Scientists know how long ago sabertooth tigers lived because of carbon dating.

When a mummy from ancient Egypt is discovered, like King Tutankhamen shown here, the date it was buried can be determined using carbon dating.

Scientists can tell how old this Tyrannosaurus Rex skeleton is using radiation dating.

Radiation and archaeology

Archaeologists are scientists that discover old items created by people. Sometimes they dig up old pots, cups, or other items. By shooting neutrons at the items, the scientists can see which atoms are in them. Then the archaeologists can figure out where the pots came from. This tells the archaeologists things like how the ancient people lived, who they traded with, and how they made the things they used. Archaeologists have dug up objects that were used by the Mayan people 1,800 years ago. Using neutrons, archaeologists know that the pots used by the Mayan people have the same type of atoms as rocks found in mines over 600 miles away. This means that the rocks used to create the pots came from that far away. That is a long distance before cars or airplanes were invented.

The same methods can be used to look at the atoms that are in other items, such as paintings. By looking at the atoms in a painting, scientists can understand what kinds of paints an artist used, and even tell if an old-looking painting is a fake.

Using radiation, archaeologist can figure out where the ancient Greeks mined the stone used to create the Parthenon.

Radiation is also able to determine how old a painting is and what types of paints are in it. This can tell us if an old painting, like this one by Dieric Bouts, is an original or a fake.

The Mayan people built pyramids like this one 1,800 years ago in Mexico. Items used by the Mayan people were made from rocks that came from over 600 miles away. Archaeologists know this by using radiation to find out what types of atoms are in the items.

Nuclear power

Radiation can be used to create electricity. When it is hit by a neutron, the nucleus of a uranium atom can split and create other atoms. This splitting is called fission. When uranium atoms split, they release lots of energy. This energy is called nuclear energy because it comes from the nucleus of an atom. Nuclear power plants turn this energy into heat inside a nuclear reactor. The nuclear reactor is usually inside a tank of water that heats up and creates steam. This steam then is turned into electricity by spinning large machines called turbines. The steam is sometimes released in large towers. About one out of every five houses in the United States gets its electricity from a nuclear power plant.

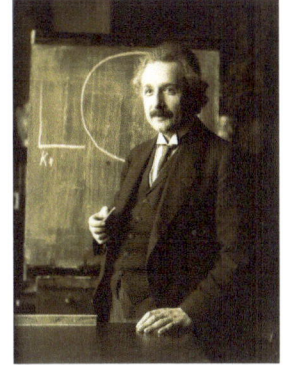

Albert Einstein's theory of relativity gave us the formula $E = mc^2$. This equation tells us that mass can be turned into energy. This is what happens in a fission reaction: some of the mass in the uranium nucleus turns to energy.

When a neutron hits a uranium nucleus, the nucleus can split into two. This fission reaction releases more neutrons and energy.

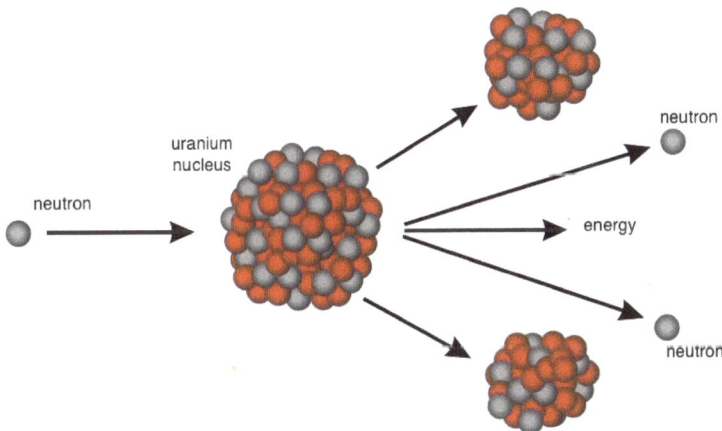

neutron

uranium nucleus

neutron

energy

neutron

This drawing shows the creation of the first man-made nuclear reactor in 1942, when scientists stacked uranium and carbon blocks to create a fission chain reaction.

When the uranium atom splits, the neutrons that it releases can then go on and cause other uranium atoms to split. This creates what is called a chain reaction because each time a uranium atom splits, the neutrons released can cause another atom to split.

Nuclear power plants require much less fuel than power plants that burn fossil fuels like coal or natural gas. A coal power plant needs to burn many train cars of coal a day. The fuel a nuclear power plant uses per year could fit inside your bedroom. Nuclear power plants do not create smoke or other air pollution and are considered to be very clean. Nuclear power does produce radiation, but it actually produces less radiation than energy produced from coal power plants. When coal is burned, there are radioactive atoms in the coal that go out of the plant as smoke.

This gray metal is uranium. When made into nuclear fuel, it can power a nuclear reactor.

Here is a nuclear power plant in Germany. The white dome is where the uranium atoms are split inside the nuclear reactor. The large towers release steam created when the heat of the reactor boils water.

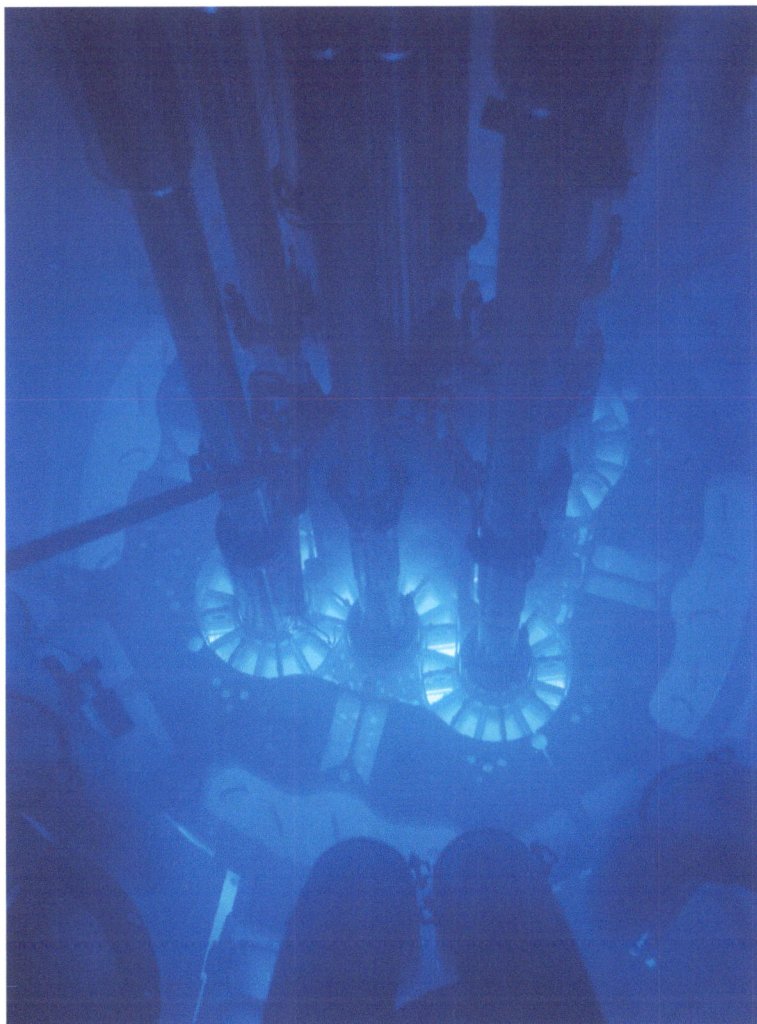

Uranium mined from the ground contains both uranium-238 and uranium-235. To make fuel for a nuclear reactor some of the uranium-238 is removed in a process called enrichment. These centrifuges spin uranium to separate uranium-238 and uranium-235.

The inside of the Advanced Test Reactor in Idaho. The fuel is at the bottom of a large pool of water. The blue glow is caused by electrons traveling near the speed of light.

This worker is inspecting a bundle of nuclear reactor fuel before it is installed in a reactor. When placed inside a reactor with several other bundles, the fission chain reaction will take place. The yellow-colored material is the uranium and the gray metal holds the fuel in place.

These are eight of the sixteen containers that hold all of the waste created by the Yankee Rowe nuclear power plant in Massachusetts over its 32 years of operation. During that time the power plant produced 44 billion kilowatt-hours of electricity. That is as much energy as 1,400,000,000 gallons of gasoline, or 195,000 train cars of coal. That many train cars would stretch from Washington, D.C. to Las Vegas.

Radiation for transportation

Nuclear power can also be used to power ships and other types of transportation. In the navy, nuclear reactors power submarines and other ships, such as aircraft carriers. The use of nuclear reactors in ships allows them to go a long time without needing more fuel. Some nuclear submarines do not need to be refueled for 25 years—the fuel lasts longer than the ship itself. Also, because nuclear reactors do not need oxygen to produce energy, these submarines can stay underwater for a long time.

Nuclear energy is also used to power spacecraft. Many of the spacecraft sent out from Earth have radioactive atoms. When these atoms decay, heat is produced, and this heat is used to produce electricity, like a nuclear battery. A common radioactive atom in these nuclear batteries is plutonium-238, which is produced in nuclear reactors. Nuclear batteries can give power for decades. The Voyager probes have been working for almost 40 years on nuclear batteries and still send messages to Earth.

Three nuclear-powered ships, USS Enterprise (bottom), USS Long Beach (center) and USS Bainbridge (top) sailing in the Mediterranean Sea. Sailors on the Enterprise are standing to form Einstein's famous equation: $E = mc^2$.

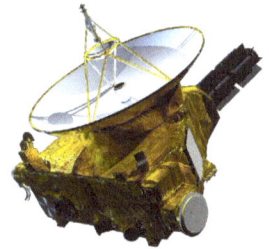

The New Horizons spacecraft traveled from Earth to Pluto in just over nine years. The spacecraft was powered by a plutonium-238 battery. The mission to Pluto was fueled by plutonium.

← This is a picture of the USS Michigan, a nuclear-powered submarine, while at a dock. This submarine could stay at sea for 90 days.

This plutonium-238 was created for a nuclear battery. It is glowing because the radiation it produces makes it hot.

Radiation in history

This plate uses uranium atoms to give it an orange color.

People did not always know that too much radiation could be dangerous. Up until 1972 you could buy plates and dishes that used radioactive uranium to make a bright orange color. Also, old glass, including some marbles, used radioactive uranium to give the glass a color. These types of atoms are not used in household items anymore.

Watches and clocks made about 100 years ago were sometimes painted with atoms of radioactive radium to make them glow in the dark. The people who painted these watches often became sick because they would wet their paintbrushes with their lips. When they did this, they accidentally ate some of the radioactive radium. These watches are not made anymore.

This watch is made with a paint containing radioactive radium.

Glass that has uranium atoms in it can glow under special lights.

Marie Curie is famous for the scientific work she did with radioactive atoms, including the discovery of radium.

Food irradiation

Many foods can spoil, or go bad, due to germs. One way to kill the germs is by shooting them with gamma rays or x–rays. This process is called food irradiation. The gamma rays and x–rays can kill any germs and bugs in the food to stop them from spoiling as easily. Gamma rays and x–rays are types of light so they do not make the food radioactive. Many spices, potatoes, meats, and grains are treated using irradiation.

In the United States, this label will be on any food that has been treated with radiation to make it more safe.

The metal device in the middle of this picture contains a radioactive substance called cobalt-60. The cobalt-60 releases gamma radiation to keep the apples fresh for longer.

Some spinach is now irradiated to kill the bacteria E. coli and keep people from getting sick.

Oil exploration

Oil is an important part of our daily lives. It is in the gasoline that powers our cars and in the plastics that make up many objects in our houses. To help find oil underground, engineers use radiation. After drilling a hole for an oil well, radioactive atoms are placed in the hole. Based on how the radiation bounces around in the ground, the engineers can then see where and how much oil is in the ground. This allows the engineers to find oil more easily and makes it less expensive for us to buy products made from oil.

When people first started looking for oil, they would dig where oil naturally came out of the ground, like in this spot. Now, with radiation, engineers can see underground to find oil.

Using radiation, engineers can get a map of where oil is located underground so that they can build oil wells like this one.

This is a ball of beryllium metal. When beryllium and americium are mixed, they create neutrons that can be used to look for oil.

Detecting radiation

People cannot see radiation. How can you know it is there? The most common way to measure, or detect, radiation is with a Geiger counter. This is a small device that makes a sound when there is radiation nearby. The number of times it makes a sound tells the user how much radiation is around. When there is a lot of radiation in the area, the detector makes a lot of fast "clicks".

This Geiger counter makes a sound when it detects radiation.

People who work around radiation, including some doctors and nurses, usually wear a special badge on their clothes called a dosimeter. The dosimeter counts the radiation that hits a person and is used to make sure that the people do not get too much radiation. Next time you are in a hospital where people get x-rays, look for the dosimeters.

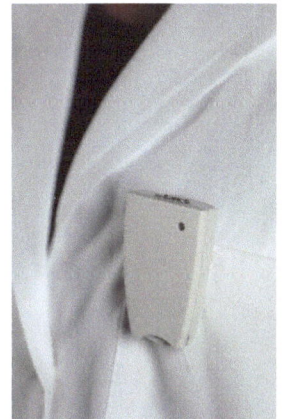

This doctor is wearing a radiation detector called a dosimeter to measure the amount of radiation he gets.

The future of radiation

Radiation has many important uses. Every year, scientists and engineers discover more uses of radiation. Currently, scientists are developing nuclear fusion that slams atoms into each other to produce energy. The slamming together of atoms creates a new, bigger atom. This is how the sun creates energy. The only fuel needed for fusion reactions, hydrogen, can be found in the water of the ocean. If people can do fusion on Earth efficiently, there may be an unlimited supply of energy and electricity.

Other new uses of radiation are being discovered all the time. Maybe you will be the scientist to discover a new use of radiation.

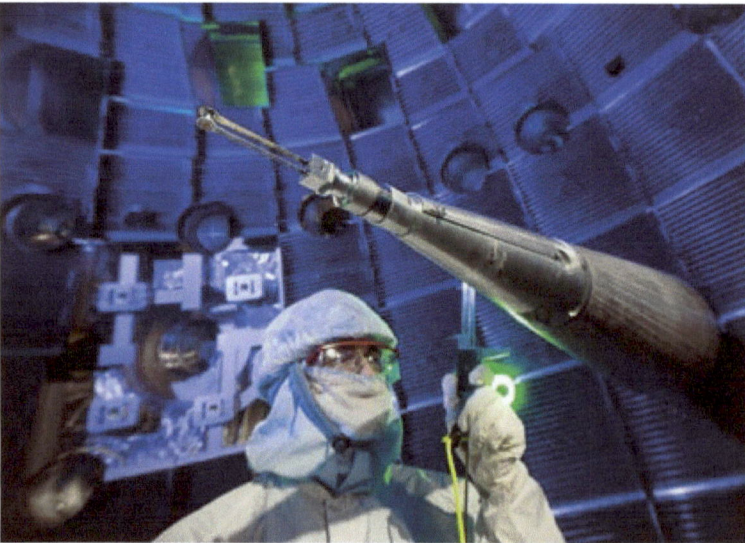

The sun is a giant nuclear reactor powered by fusion energy.

Scientists are building nuclear fusion reactors like the National Ignition Facility to slam atoms together to create energy, just like the sun does. In this reactor a giant laser heats up atoms to temperatures hotter than the sun.

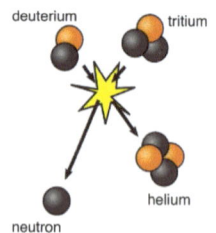

When hydrogen-2 (deuterium) hits hydrogen-3 (tritium), they can create helium and a neutron and release energy. Helium is the atom that makes balloons rise.

Glossary

americium A heavy atom created in nuclear reactors. It is used in smoke detectors. Pronounced am-mer-ee-see-um.

atom The basic building block of everything around us. Atoms are made of protons, neutrons, and electrons.

beryllium A metal whose atoms, when mixed with atoms that produce alpha radiation, like americium, can create a source of neutrons.

carbon dating The process of using the amount of radioactive carbon in something like a bone to tell how old it is.

cobalt-60 A radioactive atom that makes a large amount of gamma radiation.

decay The name for the process of a radioactive atom shooting out radiation and changing into a new atom.

dosimeter A small device for counting the amount of radiation that enters a person's body.

electron The part of the atom that flies around the outside of the nucleus.

fission When an atom splits into smaller atoms, releasing neutrons and energy.

food irradiation Using radiation to make food safer and last longer by killing germs and bugs.

fusion Combining two small atoms into a larger atom, releasing energy. The fusion of hydrogen is how the sun produces energy.

Geiger counter A tool for measuring radiation. It makes a sound when radiation is present.

hydrogen The simplest atom: it has only a single proton. Most of the hydrogen on Earth does not have a neutron in the nucleus. Some hydrogen atoms have a neutron and a proton and are called deuterium atoms. Hydrogen with two neutrons and a proton is called tritium.

neutron The part of the atom's nucleus that has a no charge.

nuclear reactor A large machine that causes uranium to fission and uses the energy from fission to create electricity.

plutonium A radioactive atom that is created in nuclear reactors when neutrons hit uranium. It is larger than uranium and does not exist naturally on Earth.

potassium An atom that is important to having a healthy body. Some potassium atoms inside of you are radioactive. Potassium is found in bananas, beans, potatoes, and other foods.

proton The part of the atom's nucleus that has a positive charge.

radioactive An atom that is not stable and will change by emitting, or shooting out, radiation.

radium A radioactive atom that is found in some rocks. The radiation from radium causes it to glow in the dark.

radon A radioactive gas that is produced naturally in the ground from radioactive uranium.

shield A material that is used to block radiation. Shields are usually thick and heavy. Lead is a common radiation shield.

thorium A radioactive element that can be found in the ground.

uranium The largest atom that is found naturally on Earth. It is radioactive and used in nuclear reactors and tank armor.

Image Credits

Below are the creators of the images used in this book listed by page and order of appearance. Where appropriate, the license under which it is used is noted. 5: Michel Wolgemut, Wilhelm Pleydenwurff / Public Domain 4: Fastfission at English Wikipedia / CC BY-SA 3.0 5: Guillaume Baffou / CC BY-SA 3.0 6 through 6: Inductiveload at Wikimedia Commons/ public domain 7: Oleg Alexandrov / Public Domain 7: Andrew Magill / CC BY 2.0 8: Jens Maus / Public Domain 8: Nevit Dilmen / CC BY-SA 3.0 8: US Navy / Public Domain 9: Bionerd at Wikimedia Commons / CC BY-SA 3.0 9: Dina Wakulchik / CC BY 2.0 10: Justus Blümer / CC BY 2.0 10: javipolinario at pixabay.com / CC0 1.0 10: Qfl247 at English Wikipedia / CC BY-SA 3.0 11: Arenamontanus at phototree.com / CC BY 2.0 11: National Institutes of Health / Public Domain 12: Neil Armstrong for NASA / public domain 12: NASA / public domain 12: Neil Armstrong for NASA / public domain 13: Dantheman9758 at English Wikipedia / CC BY 3.0 13: New York Times / Public Domain 13: David Monniaux / CC BY-SA 3.0 14: Ronny Siegel / CC BY 3.0 14: Daniel Schwen / CC BY-SA 4.0 14: Dieric Bouts / Public Domain 16: US Dept. of Energy / Public Domain 16: Heinz-Josef Lücking / CC BY-SA 3.0 DE 15: F Schmutzer / CC BY-SA 3.0 15: Stefan-Xp at Wikimedia Commons / CC BY-SA 3.0 15: Gary Sheehan (Atomic Energy Commission) / Public Domain 17: US Dept. of Energy / Public Domain 17: Argonne National Laboratory / CC BY-SA 2.0 18: RIA Novosti archive, image #132603 / Ruslan Krivobok / CC-BY-SA 3.0 18: Nuclear Regulatory Commission / Public Domain 19: US Navy / Public Domain 19: US Navy / Public Domain 19: US Dept. of Energy / Public Domain 20: Z Vesoulis / CC BY-SA 2.5 20: Wellcome Images / CC BY 4.0 20: Arma95 at Wikimedia Commons / CC BY-SA 3.0 21: United States Department of Agriculture, Food Safety and Inspection Service / public domain 21: United States Department of Energy / Public Domain 21: Victor M. Vicente Selvas / Public Domain 22: Lldenke at English Wikipedia / CC BY-SA 3.0 22: Flcelloguy at English Wikipedia / CC BY-SA 3.0 22: Aatze78 at English Wikipedia / CC BY-SA 3.0 23: US Dept. of Energy / Public Domain 23: Bullet308 at Wikimedia Commons / CC BY-SA 3.0 23: Elia.braggio at Wikimedia Commons / public domain 24: Surge 1223 at Wikimedia Commons / CC BY-SA 3.0 24: Lseaveratnif at Wikimedia Commons / CC BY 3.0

www.ingramcontent.com/pod-product-compliance
Lightning Source LLC
LaVergne TN
LVHW072110070426
835509LV00002B/105